the light in you is yours. everyone won't
understand it. people will judge, gossip,
curse, and ignore your existence. let them.
you weren't born to seek approval, you were
born to make an imprint.

you validate you.

a d r i a n   m i c h a e l

TITLES YOU MIGHT LIKE
BY
ADRIAN MICHAEL

--

loamexpressions

blinking cursor

notes of a denver native son

blackmagic

lovehues

notes from a gentle man

blooming hearts

Published by Creative Genius Publishing—
an imprint of A.Michael Ventures | Denver, CO

To contact the author visit adrianmichaelgreen.com

ISBN-13: 978-1522881292
ISBN-10: 1522881298

Printed in the United States of America

GENTLEMAN

we aren't alone, although at times the brightest sun is hidden by fog. we aren't alone. i wonder. how many out there watch strangers, or people they know, and orchestrate stories of how they probably have it all, no darkness, no fog. but in reality we all have pitch black moments, days that break our backs. aches with no names.

at times we may feel alone in traffic-jammed rooms. the storms we face are merely recycled swells sent to test our strength. we will never be alone. we all have an affinity, experiencing this life, may the current be a reminder that we are drops in the ocean bumping into each other. these are my notes. may they become part of your journey.

i choose us.
and as such
it is the most

beautifully
terrifying thing
i will always do.

—dedication

don't preoccupy yourself with how someone lives, who they love, why they do or don't do, believe or don't believe. focus on how you can be a better person.

we each have a story and our experiences shape how we perceive others and their stories. think about a place or a person that holds no judgment of your story. this person or place allows you to be your authentic self. you can show up tattered, worn, tired, messy, happy, angry, sad, embarrassed, numb, sick, hungry, weak, ashamed, hoarse, afraid, excited, lonely, confused, thirsty, any and all human emotion under the sun and moon.

go out of your way to be all of that and more for others. that takes checking in with you, some self care and self awareness.

[my thoughts]:

name that person or place you can be yourself.

the world around you can be a reflection of the world inside of you. whether you feel connected or detached, how you treat someone is a choice. & whatever rattles within, we all have our own internal battles, don't wage a war on someone else because you feel like you are losing yours.

there is an african proverb that eloquently says, "when there is no enemy within, the enemies outside cannot hurt you." chaos, the internal battle, has an easy job which is to stir as much as possible without care for who or what it is stirring but you have choice in the interpretation of that chaos. that makes all of the difference. pinpoint what bothers you and how you respond, how you treat yourself and how you treat other people. work backwards to remedy those behaviors to face your enemy head on. soon you will be free, soon the war on others will be over.

[my thoughts]:

what is your internal battle?

if you don't love them,
let them go.

i believe we hold onto people—thoughts of people, hopes of people, wants of people—as a source of comfort that can be healing for one but crippling to the other (toxic for both). you can't go on holding someone hostage for fear of being alone. if people fill your happiness and one day all went missing what would you do? how would you fill that void? it is extremely problematic when you string someone along knowing you do not care for them. it keeps them from a fulfilled life of love and happiness.

[my thoughts]:

when are you most happy?

who are you keeping away from happiness?

the light in you is yours. everyone won't understand it. people will judge, gossip, curse, and ignore your existence. let them. you weren't born to seek approval, you were born to make an imprint.

you validate you.

i sought out validation one too many times and have since vowed to walk my own path and do whatever gives me peace. such a process—allowing words and actions of others to dictate your direction—can be exhausting because not many people see you as you see you. in fact, they may even see you as a reflection of themselves and project onto you *their* own expectations of how you should think, live, act. thank them for their opinion and humbly walk into your power and validate yourself.

[my thoughts]:

what is holding you back?

i never lost hope in you.
for that to have happened hope would have needed to be
ingested. i have wandered far away from you in order to
seek hope in me.

we wrap ourselves in other people and tend to lose
ourselves.

find a way back and figure out what is needed to be
content and happy with yourself.

[my thoughts]:

what do you need?

pray for patience
your patience will be tested;
pray for love
love will manifest.

rumi, a 13th century persian poet wrote,
"what you seek is seeking you" which basically
translates into what you put out into the universe
will come to you. it has a magical way of finding
you. take patience and love for example. in your
head you may see what you want one way but what
you get looks a bit off-color. challenging.

what you ask for isn't going to come in a pretty
bow or have a label on it. it will be random and
discrete.

you will be tested and faced with opportunity to
see how you receive it and unfold it.

[my thoughts]:

what do you pray/meditate/ask for?

good hearts always need an outlet.

i cried into the wind, a soul cleansing kind of cry, one night in oklahoma. i remember it vividly. i walked until i stumbled upon a water fountain about five minutes from my apartment. a tall cascading bronze bear frozen on all fours looked over her two tiny cubs as they played in the falling water.

cars would rush by and embedded their steel drum sounds into the whirl of wind and the woosh of water. my colorado tears harmonized. my heart was heavy; my heart needed a release.

oddly, it felt like she too was watching over me. reminding me that i was not alone, that i could cry into the wind and she would be there to watch and listen.

[my thoughts]:

when was your last soul cry?

she practices being herself everyday. having to shed the layers of other identities took time. she even lost friendships. she couldn't fill their egos anymore.

when you focus on yourself, spend time with yourself, and love yourself, some relationships have to go.

[my thoughts]:

how do you practice being yourself?

*i don't have the answers and i don't pretend to profess
that i do. but i will search for perspective and attempt to
make dents to unlearn the false truths i've been taught.*

too often we consume what we see and hear
as accurate definitions, standards and norms.
happiness resides outside those boundaries; create
your own existence, discover your truth.

[my thoughts]:

what do you know for sure?

let love in.
don't be a stone wall.

at some point in your life something happened.
a traumatic event or series of unforunate events
has covered you, trampled you. conscious or
unconscious things, people, and or behaviors now
block you from letting love in. how far back can
you trace it? can you locate the root? think. maybe
you already know. perhaps at first glance you
glossed it with a brush and deemed it meaningless,
but take a look at it, again. and again. you were
innocent and open and you were undeserving
of those ugly words, those hateful hands, that
dreadful resistance, his blank stares, her lies, their
absence. zero in on every aspect of your life and
find healing, or you will forever be formidable and
stuck.

[my thoughts]:

what is stopping you from love?

you are on a path to outgrow certain parts of yourself that have traveled with you long enough; don't analyze it or you'll advocate to keep what you don't need. what's good for you will go with you, let that other stuff shed naturally.

easier said than done? mark banschick, psychiatrist and child advocate, says that people hold onto things for many reasons such as lack of permission, fear, and that they may need it someday. what is your reason? holding onto "stuff" has an underlying control factor that is filling, letting go is scary and requires vulnerability. can holding on be pyschological, especially the bad "stuff"? roy f. baumeister, a professor of social psychology at florida state university believes so. according to him, "bad emotions…and bad feedback have more impact than good ones. bad impressions and bad stereotypes are quicker to form and more resistant to disconfirmation than good ones." bad things outweigh the good, and that shouldn't be the case. let go. set fire to negativity and dance in its smoke.

[my thoughts]:

what are you holding onto?

her purpose is simple.

love herself. love others.

a rebel lives inside of you. and resents the times you look both ways for approval. that part of you that wants to go a little crazy is aching for adventure. unlatch what holds you back, let go of that fear. break that box of rules that detains your soul. at least once, darling. at least once.

here's a permission piece. a hall pass of sorts, but for an unlimited amount of time——use as advertised, if not for you, for the rebel inside of you. echoed by esteemed author elizabeth gilbert, "your soul has been waiting for you to wake up to your own [rebellious]* existence for years." live. have fun. release.

* my notated addition

[my thoughts]:

why do you seek approval?

your words become worthless
the moment you use him
rather than love him.

humans have a way of letting our wants blind us
to what we actually need and all the while, people
in our lives can become collateral damage. we
sometimes use and misuse to fill a temporary gap.
think about a moment you felt used, really felt
mistreated. and the hurt that arised, the blisters
that grew on your heart. how did it feel to know
you were giving them your all and you only
received the bare minimum in return? it's okay
to take advantage of someone only if you desire
to water and grow with them, when you see and
honor them for what they teach you and what you
teach them.

[my thoughts]:

when have you felt used?

you hid. for far too long. from a world that was afraid of its own shadow. you came out from darkness and realized that the world was actually hiding from you.

to hide, both literally and figuratively, imprisons the soul. worst part is this is self-selected. we give our power to others and say, "here, take my life, i'll just go sit in the corner. you need me more than i need me." how sad. michelle d'avella, a mentor and breathwork teacher writes, "we all need to be seen. it's part of what makes us human. when we don't allow ourselves to be seen, we diminish our importance in this world. we undervalue ourselves. we hold ourselves back from greatness. we stifle our contributions." show up, be your true self regardless of what the world thinks, we are better for it, you are better for it.

[my thoughts]:

what are you hiding from?

she is exhausted. she is fed up. no longer will she tolerate being treated less than wild.

your expectations of her to change have wilted her desire to adhere to her animal instincts she forgot to honor the universe. the further you pull her back to her self she will remember who she left.

[my thoughts]:

who / what is keeping you from your self?

i often wonder about the masks i wear. if i own more than one. if and when i switch out one for another.

we are built in parts. segments with different functions. i believe my surroundings require a certain level of energy and degrees of personality that dictate how i show up. if you want me to be outgoing, i can be. if you need me to be strong, i can be. if you wish i was like water, i can be. if you desire me to be like somebody else, i can't be. how you see me is dictated on who i show you. i am a three-act play re-writing my script. constantly working to be the best version of me: my characters may shift between scenes but this skin is my only mask that i cannot take off.

[my thoughts]:

what mask(s) do you wear?

when you feel like giving up
and laying in defeat, trust in your love.

remember the reason you began this journey.
nothing will come easy. effort requires discomfort.
push through. dig deep. love is only worth it if you
fight for it.

[my thoughts]:

what does love mean to you?

are you willing to fight for it?

flow with energy. you are made full of its magic.
be mindful of who you share it with.

no one owns your magic but you. you might share
its ingredients or give some of it away. but the
beautiful and tragic has been your super power
since always. you can't get rid of it even if you
tried; your magic is a precious gift.

[my thoughts]:

do you believe in your magic?

i get it. you're not one to share your feelings. i don't know if you've been hurt before, lead astray by a two-bit-hustler. or maybe you've never seen euphoria in the form of another living being. whatever it is. give this a chance. just because you don't have a name for it, doesn't mean you should deny its existence.

when we deny, we push. when we push, we create distance. any time spent with someone, no matter the frequency, is a relationship (i say that time and time again) and communication is a huge chunk of it—if you want it to work and be healthy. this takes sacrificing your fear, your judgment, your anxiety, your hesitation, and trust in its process. hurt is real. we all have experienced different levels of it but challenge yourself to feel it out, work it out, love it out.

[my thoughts]:

what or who are you not giving a chance?

who did you give a chance?

there are three sides to love—pleasure, lust and torment.

i believe we experience each on different
frequencies. sometimes all at once, sometimes
not at all. you may not believe in it, love may have
been exiled and abolished, but it's there, waiting
to be asked to dance again. you can't give what
you don't have nor can you catch what you don't
see, but love is a hopeful dream with eyes wide
open. i thought love didn't exist, that it had died,
but it rested patiently, dormant and quiet, for me
to bring it back to life. and that has to be true for
you, too. you have to revive it for yourself. try
looking at love differently, redefine it. perhaps love
can be anything you want it to mean. here is my
definition, if i may:

love is.
let it be.
like wine,
let it breathe.

[my thoughts]:

what did love look like before?

what does love look like now?

what i needed then
i don't need now.

a favorite professor of mine, maw-der foo, had
us re-examine abraham maslow's 1943 theory
of human motivation my senior year in college.
maslow states that humans have basic needs, and
once those needs are met we seek to fulfill the
next need in a hierarchal fashion, and that our
most basic needs must be met prior to elevating
or reaching for a higher growth need. those needs
are:
  1. physiological - air, food, shelter, sex, sleep
  2. safety - protection from the elements, law,
     security, stability
  3. social - intimacy, love, belongingness, friendship,
     affection
  4. esteem - achievement, respect for self, respect from
     others, independence
  5. self-actualization - realizing personal potential, self-
     fulfillment
that management class turned out to be more
about managing myself, rather than soley the
management of others, i realize in hindsight.

[my thoughts]:

what is it that you *really* need?

sometimes
we have to face
what is wrong for us, with us
before we can adjust
and discover
what is right for us.

life is all about experiences and making meaning
out of them. if you never experience you never
learn, you never grow, your world is minimal.
the path can be grueling but worth it and beautiful
if you take one step at a time knowing that you
will stumble sometimes, fall sometimes, glide
sometimes, slip sometimes, crash sometimes.
discovering what is right for us also takes self
analysis, self inventory. like the talented novelist
james baldwin once said, "not everything that is
faced can be changed, but nothing can be changed
until it is faced."

[my thoughts]:

when was the last time you faced difficulty?

weep often. not in sadness.
but in celebration.
for things to grow water must fall.

crying can be cathartic. healing. make room for
tears as a way to cleanse your soul.

[my thoughts]:

what are you afraid of?

don't confuse a hard shell with toughness.

sometimes it's for their own protection.

silence is a messenger. listen.

silence speaks, as spiritualist eckhart tolle puts it.
what is your relationship with silence? silence used
to scare me because i didn't know how to interpret
its language. i *misinterpreted* it by assuming i was
bored and had to fill the absence of sound with
sound, or movement, or... something. i decided
to face my relationship with silence and ask myself
why i felt so uneasy about it, why it made me feel
uncomfortable. i realized what i was doing. silence
was a messenger from my inner self that i ignored
to my own fear of inquisition, not knowing or
understanding what i wanted when i felt bored or
restless. tolle says, "you can stay bored and restless
and observe what it feels like to be bored and
restless. as you bring awareness to the feeling, there
is suddenly some space and stillness around it. a
little at first, but as the sense of inner space grows,
the feeling of boredom will begin to diminish in
intensity and significance. so even boredom can
teach you who you are and who you are not."

[my thoughts]:

in the absence of noise, who are you?

i relieved the guard that stood watch in front of my heart.

his post was no longer needed. for years weeds spiked the bars in front of its high walls. it was going to be me. just me this time. as i let myself feel again a rush of intense light blinded me and the gauntlet began. i had to face my own fears. my own demons. my own stuff. & i'm still fighting. fighting to find my true self. maybe not the perfect. maybe not the best. but the version i can be at peace with.

[my thoughts]:

what are you guarding yourself from?

my fear that they won't love me,
which is just a protection of my
deepest fear being that I won't
love myself.

settle for a love
that will whip you into greatness;
if you fall short of greatness
you'll still be loved.

love is a circle. it operates on need, not want. as you redefine what love means, love itself has need. love requires integrity—the alignment of what you say and what you do—to be fully functional. your words and your actions must line up. this is its only request. when you enter into love's contract, you are entering a promise to give it your all, to give your best, to try, to fight.

[my thoughts]:

are you fulfilling love's promise?

and when the wall crumbled, her life was transformed;
assassins of character can no longer breach the soul of a
warrior.

emotional walls take work to get through,
especially if someone is interested in being let in.
but you won't let that happen, or atleast, you won't
let that be easy. with good reason. author galit
breen provides four truths about women who put
up emotional walls:

1) to manage what happens next
2) it's an easy defense mechanism
3) when you put up walls today, you are
   acting like the person you once were
4) emotional walls come from a legitimate
   place

you are a soul warrior that must (re)commit
yourself, to yourself. it will be uncomfortable,
work through it. as breen advises, so do i: this hard,
uncomfortable work, can only be done by you.

[my thoughts]:

what needs to happen for your wall to come down?

a defense mechanism:
defending myself from myself

dear self,
we have today to re-energize
and find peace. start, continue,
or finish yesterday's task.

take time to be with your thoughts & meditate.
tomorrow doesn't exist yet.

[my thoughts]:

what is it that you *really* need to work on?

love,
it's not a race
take it slow
we are
icicles
clenched
on fenches
soon to be
puddles
on the ground

enjoy love. *be* in love.

[my thoughts]:

how is your relationship with love?

they know your triggers.
what sets you off.
detonate those land mines.
work through your own mess.

relationships fail for many reasons: unreadiness,
immaturity, season, irreconcilable differences,
incompatibility, timing, infidelity, self-sabotage,
them-sabotage, mistrust, misleading, and mental,
physical, or emotional distress. the list goes on.

those patterns leave trails. remnants of where we
have been and how we conduct ourselves leaves
marks on all who we encounter along the way.
analyze your patterns—who you've loved, how
you've loved, how you acted, how they acted—
why did it work? why didn't it work?

if *you* are a battle field covered in land mines, you
will easily be set off. nothing will last or be healthy
if you don't work through your war zone.

[my thoughts]:

what triggers you?

not being championed
stood-up for

pain never really goes away.
the sting may leave but the scar will take time to fade.
you may not see it, the wound is no longer visible.
reminders of what happened, reminders of how it
happened, will linger.

be patient with the healing process. be active
during the healing process. for it is what you do
with your time that will make all of the difference.
time itself will not heal you, you must heal you
within the ticks of each moment. name the pain
you feel, give it a color, determine its sound,
locate it in your body, foreclose its residence. yes,
it will be terrifying, facing the trauma, but if you
don't confront history, it will continue to poison
you. maya angelou put it frank: history, despite
its wrenching pain, cannot be unlived, but if faced
with courage, need not be lived again.

courage + time + soul work = healing.

[my thoughts]:

have you taken the time to heal?

a game of madness—

phases. we go through them. doing what we think
others approve of. closing ourselves off to do what
we want. the pull of each is different in us all. we
grapple with it. somewhere on that line.
searching. to live for others. to live for ourselves.

a game of madness for those who decide to play.

obey your soul & be true to your heart.
find your purpose. live your purpose.

[my thoughts]:

what is your purpose?

a woman will make it clear if she wants nothing to do with you. watch for her cues. pick up on the subtleties. she isn't into games but is holding out to make sure you aren't just playing the field.

when she gives you her heart
she is committed to you and only you.

[my thoughts]:

what game(s) do you play?

why try when you have someone
you don't have to try with?

does this situation sound familiar?—you like
someone, but they play extremely hard to get
or are completely uninterested. someone likes
you but you won't give them the time of day. the
person you want to be with treats you terribly
and in turn you treat the person that wants you
similarly without even knowing it (or knowingly).
ring a bell? am i close?

whatever the case may be, your all will never be
enough to someone that doesn't see or appreciate
you. there is an amazing person just inside your
reach who is compatable and worthy of the light
you willingly share. look up.

[my thoughts]:

who is it that you don't have to try with?

trust your senses.
allergies flare
around poisonous
people.

you'll know when someone isn't good for you
when you let them into your world and there are
negative side effects. you can't put a finger on it.
you become ill. unhealthy. the moment you push
them out and cleanse your environment, you are
whole again. healthy.

the true test will be how often you let that same
person (or type of person) into your life.

[my thoughts]:

who are you allergic to?

how do you plan to cleanse your environment?

as seasons and tastes change so do appetites.

new cars. new phones. new deals.
they come out every year. think about it.
there is an infatuation with the next best thing.
as seasons and tastes change so do appetites.
they get bigger.

no wonder relationships don't last.

what you did to get her won't always be what you
need to keep her. as people change, our needs
change. pay attention and treat her accordingly.

having a high lover turnover rate is not a good thing.

[my thoughts]:

what is the best constant in your life?

sometimes we snap and can't contain ourselves.
while others rush to fix you, i long for these moments
and honor such courage when you break into pieces.

fall apart and stay there, please.
& when you're ready
i am here if you need me.

if you feel like being still, be still.
sit in silence and be.
be in that moment.
absorb that space.
sink into all the matter around you.
notice the peace in stillness.

love can be a stillness. love can enter our being and calm us down. it can also be unnerving, when it thrusts itself (with the best of intentions) into parts of our selves we never knew existed. or creates extreme sensations we don't remember ever sensing or have never never felt). love is a reminder. sit with it. feel it. absorb it. sink into it.

love is an equalizer, a neutralizing substance that fosters peace in a mind-body-soul-world possibly interrupted with chaos.

be still, dear heart.

[my thoughts]:

when was the last time you were still?

no part of us is accessory.
we can't be loved separately.

parts of us want to be seen. no desire, no ambition
to be made a big deal. being noticed. being
acknowledged. that is it. that is all that matters.
to ignore even one ounce of who we are or what
we reveal is to weaken our humanity.

[my thoughts]:

what is important to you?

i won't apologize
for exiting toxic wastelands.
my mental space
requires this of me.

love is stillness and peace. if you aren't getting
that, go. depart. walk away. or atleast pull back
your loving energy and hold onto your investment.
everything about you is valuable, you provide value.
toxic people, toxic circumstance, toxic energy
brings down that value and is completely damaging.
dr. sherrie bourg carter says, "unhealthy
relationships can turn into a toxic *internal*
environment that can lead to stress, depression,
anxiety, and even medical problems." is your health
important? of course it is! i am glad we agree.
simply ask yourself two simple questions:

am i happy?
am i healthy?

[my thoughts]:

what are your requirements?

love is vibration.
a connection of the highest frequency.
we can try to wrap our minds to define it
but love is ever evolving,
constantly transforming.

move with it. feel with it. grow with it.
dive into its rhythm. breathe its air.
become the vibration. become full.
become love. let it cover all of you.

[my thoughts]:

how have you transformed?

*lessons in love will only take root
when you're ready to listen.*

many years ago i was having dinner outside of
downtown denver with one of my closest friends
from high school at a place called *las delicias*. we
talked about what boys typically talk about: sports,
jobs, family, and relationships. mostly always about
relationships. the center of that conversation was
around my relationship, more specifically,
my relationship with relationships. let me explain.

up to that point i had been spending time with
people. nothing lasted. nothing serious. i wasn't
ready for commitment, for a relationship. what he
told me was life changing: "it sounds like you have
an issue with boundaries," he said. "spending time
with someone *is* a relationship!" but i never saw it
that way. i didn't think of it that way. i was having
mini relationships and didn't even know it—
entering contracts without really understanding
the fine print. *my soul was given some delicious food for
thought.*

[my thoughts]:

what is the best lesson love has ever taught you?

do what makes you happy
and become the happiness
that you find

only you can locate the source.

[my thoughts]:

no, really, are you happy?

if you force it
you have to be willing to
accept if it doesn't work out.

force, by definition, is about power, control, persuasion—verb. to compel, constrain or oblige (oneself or someone) to do something. and what happens when we force someone to do something, say something, be something that they don't want, or push ourselves into what we don't want? pain and sadness. unfulfillment. guilt. resentment. anamosity. regret. all follow.

why is force even necessary? i suppose if one person wants a love so bad they should be persistant but *only* if they have permission of a willing heart they so badly wish to pursue. persist in the *act* of finding what you deserve. you cannot force anything that is not meant to be. try a little tenderness, otis redding urged in song.

don't force it. be tender. be gentle.

[my thoughts]:

why do you force things?

everything worth having
doesn't always come easy.
you must fight for it.
and they must be willing
to fight for you.

when we are in this, really in this, we prepare for
hardship. embrace hardship. it's part of the deal.
hardship is an activator, a catalyst that encourages
tenacity, patience, and courage. it will feel like
fire, walking on hot coals, swimming in smoke,
breathing angry fumes. it makes you stronger. but
it's natural to jump out of the hot seat at first—the
only thing hot that you like is your tea, coffee,
and bath. yet, wait a second. don't you let those
cool down before you experience its reunion with
you? treat your relationship just the same, fire has
a range of temperatures. honor its flames. see the
heat as a test. fight through it.

love will be tested. love is a test.

[my thoughts]:

how has love tested you?

wake up in love.
breathe in love.

how is my mind?
how is my body?
how is my soul?

i ask these questions of myself to check in. if my
actions are distant, if my words are unkind, if my
energy is neglectful, there is imbalance. most of
which can be rooted in environment, circumstance,
relationship. *thoughts become things* (as the old saying
goes) and such truth will show up in the spaces we
operate in, so what we put out we will get back in
return. what we consume, we become. so return
to yourself, back to the basics (you are far from
basic), and produce love, breathe love, be love. for
love is healing.

[my thoughts]:

what are you putting out into the universe?

let them go crazy.
maintain your peace.

do some breath work.
short, steady, deep, breaths.
calm yourself.
drop your shoulders, release the weight.
unclench your stomach, breathe outwardly.
take in more air, feel its cool. taste its freshness.
notice your thoughts, let them whiz by.
return back to your breath.
settle your feet, center them on the ground.
sense vibrations from head to toe.
empty your mind.
fill your heart.
control the pace of your breath.
push negativity out of your galaxy.

[my thoughts]:

when are you the most peaceful?

comparing another journey to your own
is not a fair assessment of where you are
or where you should be.

to say you are behind tricks the mind to believe the biggest lie. let milestones be set at your own pace.

in 2015 approximately 1.96 billion people had registered on a variety of social media platforms (the top 5 being facebook, pinterest, instagram, twitter and linkedin). in 2016 that number is estimated to jump up to 2.13 billion. currently there are 7.3 billion humans on earth which means almost 30% of the population is on a social network. we know how easy it is to get sucked into what others are doing in comparison to ourselves. social media is not reality. if you find yourself anxious, stressed, overwhelmed, angry, or any variety of unease (and are an avid user of a virtual world) unplug. let go. take care of you. don't absorb pixels as vitamins.

[my thoughts]:

when was the last time you compared yourself to yourself?

they found the recipe to get your attention. the days and weeks you sob inside shackled with agony is forgotten when they give you a teaspoon of sugar. a sliver of what they know you want. hope now rests on your heart but it shrivels up when they don't utter a sound. you sob and curl into sadness. you send one-way messages and stare at blank responses. you are waiting for someone who doesn't want you. they get off on your self-suffering. it hypes their ego while they're out with someone else.

give yourself the biggest gift and walk away from self-destruction and walk into self-love. loving you first will be a life-long fix.

[my thoughts]:

do you enjoy suffering?

she is known for making fires

with her smile.

sometimes walking away and releasing someone
you love back into the wild world is best.

even if you give all you have, sometimes you can't
give them what they need. be responsible. someone
out there is better suited to love them. and it will
hurt. you will break and feel broken. but if you
hold onto them (no matter how tight) in the core
of your souls you both may resent one another.

this is maturity.

[my thoughts]:

who/what do you need to let go of?

never underestimate the power of a small gesture.

the tiniest star can light up a room. going above and beyond isn't always necessary when a hug, a smile, a handwritten note, will be just fine.

[my thoughts]:

what is one thing you can do right now to make
you smille? to make someone else smile?

love is about being there when most needed,
not so much when it comes easy.
hardship requires attention, not distance.

practice makes perfect. isn't that how that phrase goes? with doing something over and over again there is an automatic assumption that you get better at that thing. in many instances i argue that as you get better in one area, you are substantially getting worse in another. take avoidance for example. if you practice avoiding difficult conversations, congratulations! you become an avoider. if you practice leaving, props! you become absent. so flip it. if you avoid, if you leave, practice the complete opposite. determine what it is about challenge that you find uncomfortable and face them. courage is the practice of staring hardship in the eyes alongside fear and conquering difficulty, together.

[my thoughts]:

if you run away when it gets hard, why?

if you stay do you make things worse, why?

steps you will take to be present:

what you have is special. and it is not like previous engagements. you found someone that complements you. whole souls destined to collide. but you hit a stumbling block, a rocky road.

you have doubts. you thought this one was it. that this one was your match. that this one would not give you pain or be difficult. every path isn't paved and this one is no different. they make you better but the temperature is rising. parts of you want to run and this is where you make a choice. are you willing to leave in hopes to find an easier path? what looks greener on the surface doesn't always have better soil. stay and bear witness to meaningful growth in you and in them.

[my thoughts]:

are you willing to make it work? why or why not?

mend weak relationships or let them go. toxic people
are meant to poison your energy. it's up to you who you
breathe in.

i want to surround myself with supportive
energy. uplifting vibes. positive affirmation. this
world, along with myself, is far from perfect, yet
i encourage constructive feedback. that is very
different from negativity. negative attitudes are
void of growth mindset. it is like a heavy fog that
infects your lungs. you can't breathe. in fact, people
with funky attitudes want to spread their bad juju
and pollute all things they touch. negativity has
thick roots. be cautious. it can latch itself onto you.
it rears its head not just in people, but in places and
things.

if you fuel it, you become it.

[my thoughts]:

what type of people do you breathe in?

she tells you she doesn't want to talk but her body language says otherwise. prod her a bit. check to see what is really bothering her. kiss her on her forehead and assure her that when she's ready to talk, you'll be there to listen. a gentle man gives her time, space, and attention.

if a woman says "nothing" when asked what is wrong, what does she *really* mean? chelsia toon gives some helpful perspective. toon writes, "she has high hopes of you being perceptive, try to rise to the occasion. if you find yourself truly helpless in doing so, channel your efforts into appearing sensitive and smart." that's the mind reading piece. she continues by reminding us that by saying "nothing" she may not be ready to talk about it at that point in time. honor that. "nothing" can also mean that nothing is wrong.

[listen to her body]

[my thoughts]:

when does body language create a barrier for you?

you may look good on the outside but i am more
interested in what you look like on the inside.

we like to decorate the outside of our bodies—
tattoos, clothes, jewelry, the works. some of those
very things are what others may find attractive
about us. but now it is time to go below the
surface. outward appearance can be a brutal facade.
layers of masks distract us. perhaps even allow us
to overcompensate. or maybe those very things
we wear on our skin is what our souls wish to
radiate. we tell stories with our bodies by presence
and appearance. think about how you show up. be
mindful and aware of the stories you are sharing.
when our spirit aligns with our physical body,
magic happens. it's like you have found the sweet
spot of life. you harmonize with the universe.

he wanted to know her on a deeper level,
so he studied her soul.

[my thoughts]:

how do you look on the inside?

lovers need reassurance, not excuses.
by being truthful you build trust.
lying digs holes you can't get out of.

here you are. it's just you and you. you need to
come to an understanding, a mutual agreement.
it is time to examine and unlearn some logical
fallacies you have taught yourself. think back to
your most recent lie (or you can call it a fib) and
critically analyze the reason you decided to lie/
fib. what did you come up with? self-preservation,
dignity, protection, just because, no reason…?
all possible. all human. this is what german
philosopher friedrich nietzshe said about it:
the lie is a condition of life. what do you think?
let that marinate.

is the truth that hard? i suppose the truth can be a
formidable mountain. dreadful. scary. discouraging.
(side note: yes, we never intentionally want to
hurt others if that indeed is the reason we avoid
telling the truth). and what about the lies we tell
ourselves? what damage does that cause? hmm.

[my thoughts]:

why do you lie?

love can be like glass
handle with care

jhené aiko efuru chilombo points out an incredible observation in her song "lyin king," that goes like this:

> okay, so you just
> go around breaking hearts
> just to see what is inside;
> go around stealing them
> feeding them to your pride.
> did you ever stop and think that
> i might really need that
> to stay alive?

everything we say, everything we do, has meaning. no matter how big, no matter how small. letting someone into your life is far from meaningless. let alone letting someone into your heart. it is okay to be curious but if we continuously detach value of precious objects then love and relationships will no longer be held sacred and taken seriously.

[my thoughts]:

honestly, have you ever broken a heart just to see
what was inside? has it happened to you?

O

when she lets you in

protect her heart.

how far am i willing to bend before i break? and how much time can i give up to accommodate unhealthy situations?

we sacrifice a lot when it comes to red flags (things that people do that make you tilt your head, squint your eyes, and grit your teeth) and we throw them under the rug as a way to shrug it off and forget. we all have baggage and mannerisms that may not bode well with who we want to be with. if you don't talk about what bothers you, then you run the risk of accumulating negative emotions that will poke holes in your relationship. that rug won't be able to contain everything you sweep under there. at some point you have to address red flags. communication is queen.

[my thoughts]:

what is a red flag that you haven't addressed yet?

spending time with someone,
no matter the frequency,
is a relationship.
fine print determines if it is platonic or intimate.
regardless of the title you place on it,
be cautious. be aware. be kind.
the energy you give to someone is a gift.

don't lead someone anywhere you yourself
wouldn't dare go.

[my thoughts]:

what are your intentions with this person?

where are you now in the relationship?
where do you want to go?

practice saying yes more than you say no.

take time to try new things with your partner, even if you don't want to. the moment is worth it because you are with your beloved. and if you really don't want to, if you feel uncomfortable or unsafe, let your lover know.

[my thoughts]:

what do you need to practice more of?

maybe she's holding out for a love that doesn't exist yet.

i have always admired patience. there is no rush. there is no worry. it's a calm demeanor. as if somehow they know or have faith to know that eventually if something is meant to be, it will be. in some cases a patient person might not get in the way of themselves and consciously decides to wait. this does not mean they stop living. in fact, a patient person by nature is adventurous and open-minded. patience has taught them to (as poet rudyard kipling exclamated) wait and not be tired by waiting. they know what they want and will not settle for anything short of it.

[signs]

[my thoughts]:

what are you waiting for?

water her.
even if
the sun
droughts
your well.

like cars need gas and plants need sun, we need
nourishment. find ways to fill yourself.

[unselfish]

[my thoughts]:

what fills you? who fills you?

if you separate flaw from beauty and
treat them differently that is not love.

that is bias. blend both flaw and beauty into one
lens and see them as they are.

accept them as they are. and when either beauty
or flaw shows its face you will just see the one
you adore.

[my thoughts]:

what does unconditional love mean to you?

good hearts always find a way to exist in hardship.

her rose-colored glasses were shattered by steel-toed boots and handed back to her as if she was responsible for her own innocence being taken. broken relationship after broken relationship she shined her heart and swept up her pieces with a dust pan. do not pity her. don't you dare coddle her wounds. she is a warrior princess worthy of her weight in gold and finds strength in picking herself up.

so stop thinking she's broken and appreciate her mosaic—what we think is shattered is merely an artist unscrambling and evolving into her true self, blending both dark and golden shadows.

[my thoughts]:

how do you exist in hardship?

love is not just a feeling, love is a state of mind.

love is a gravitational pull that ties beautiful souls
to exist with one another. it is never perfect and
it takes a lot of work. love is a commitment, a
journey not for the faint of heart. surrender to its
magic, don't resist its charm. whatever you do and
wherever you go, love will always be your guide.

[my thoughts]:

how do you practice loving yourself?

how do you practice loving others?

if you don't know their love language,
you aren't paying attention.

gary chapman identified five ways to express and
experience love:

* gifts
* quality time
* words of affirmation
* acts of service
* physical touch

know which language(s) speak to you. become
fluent in the language(s) that speak to your partner.

[my thoughts]:

what is your love language?

what is your partner's love language?

love, like a pencil,
should be sharpened.

together, let's break our hearts.
plant the pieces at the highest peak
and let the sky breathe us in.
when we become clouds that sprawl above us,
may they hold the collective essence of our soul.
reminding us that we are one heart. one love. one world.

GENTLEMAN

COOL RUNNINGS
IN DARK TUNNELS

a novel

BY ADRIAN MICHAEL
COMING SOON

Made in the USA
San Bernardino, CA
22 April 2020

68993713R00100